Super Panda

Jessica Hartshorn

To Charles and Zara from Jessica Hartshorn

First Print Edition 2020

Copyright Jessica Hartshorn

This book is dedicated to Bella, Bethany and Tom.

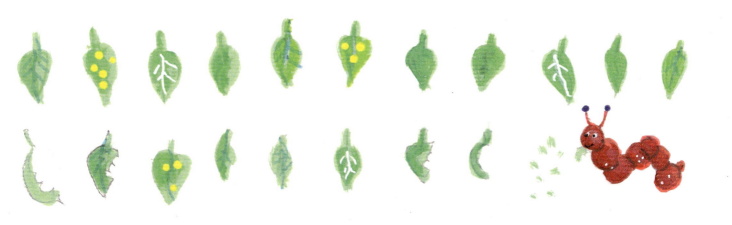

In the leafy jungle a party is about to begin.....

..... a fabulous fancy dress party.

Panda Paul is getting ready... ready to become.... Super Panda!

'Look at my special cape made of giant, green, jungle leaves,' said Paul. 'Mummy has stitched and sewn all day to create it!

Now I'm extraordinarily super.'

'It's a long way to the party,' thought Paul. 'I'd better fly!'

So off he ran through the leafy jungle, with his cape flying behind.

But was he all alone?

'What is that sound?' said Super Panda Paul. 'Maybe it's the silver fish?'
'Silver fish, was that you?'

'No, no, no! The silver fish go SPLASH, SPLASH, SPLASH.'

So Paul continued deeper into the leafy jungle in search of the fabulous fancy dress party.

Paul zooms and zigs, zigs and zooms past the tall trees.

MUNCH, MUNCH, MUNCH.

'What is that sound?' mumbled Paul. 'Is it the blue birds flying high?'

'No, no, no. The blue birds go
SWOOSH, SWOOSH, SWOOSH.

'Never mind, onwards the leaf Paul zigs and zooms

...aid Paul as he sped deeper into ...ungle to find the fabulous fancy dress party.

...zooms and zigs through the leafy jungle.

Super Panda Paul reaches a clearing, where the grass is green, the flowers smell sweet and the sun shines bright.

'Lion??? AHHHH'

Paul looked up. 'Phew, it's not a lion, it's a big creepy cloud. I wasn't scared! But what is that sound??'

As Paul glanced across the leafy jungle, he could see he had nearly reached the fabulous fancy dress party.

He zigs and zooms, zooms and zigs, rolls and wriggles, twists and turns through the leafy jungle.

As he bounded across the log bridge, he could hear the jungle music.

The party was in full swing. Lots of jungle animals were there....

Emily Elephant was dressed as an excellent elf

Jim and John the jungle chimps looked cheeky as clowns.

Lenard the lizard was dressed as a lively lifeguard.

Betty the bear danced beautifully as a ballerina.

As Paul arrived at the party....
All the animals looked puzzled.
'I'm here! Don't I look super?'
shouted Paul.

'Paul,' said Emily. 'Where is your costume?'

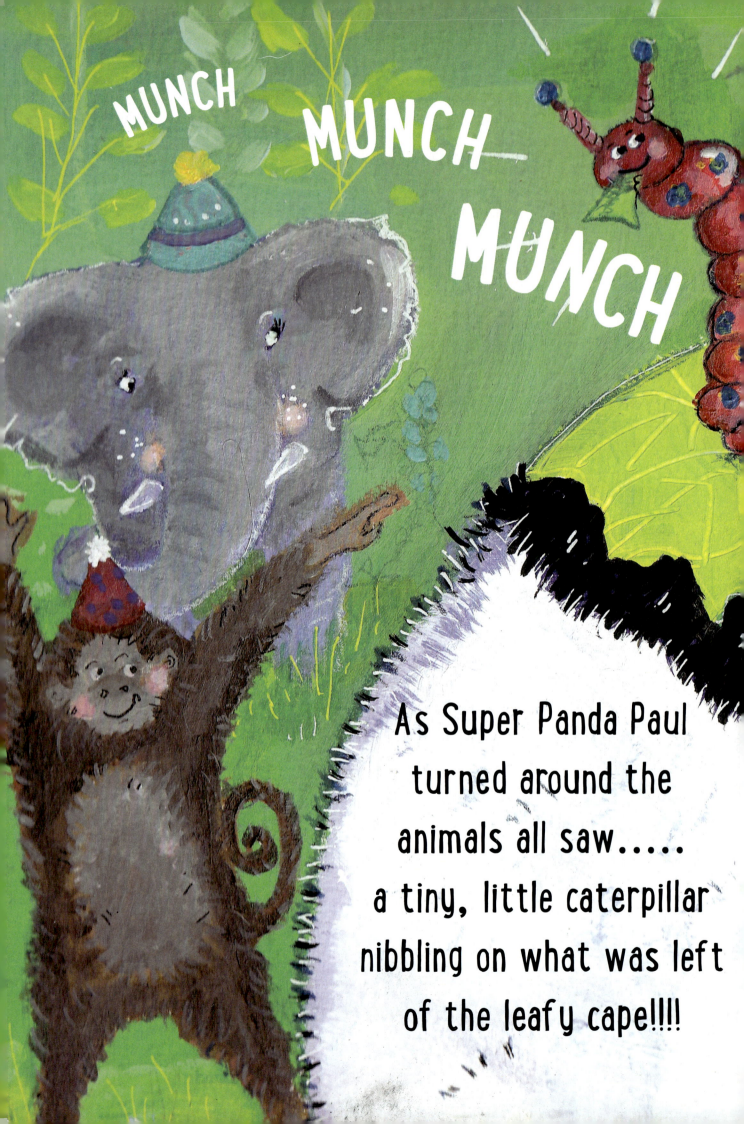

'Never mind Paul, you don't need a cape to be a Super Panda,' said Betty Bear.

'You are always super to us.'

They danced the night away in the leafy jungle.....

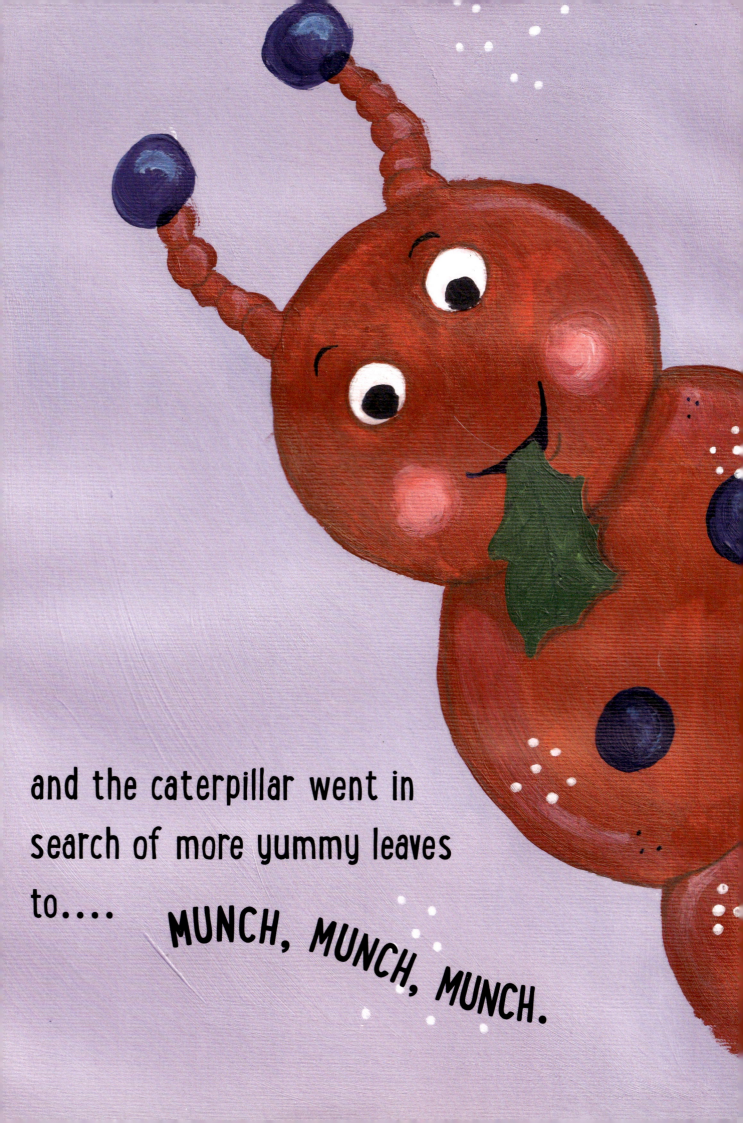

and the caterpillar went in search of more yummy leaves to.... MUNCH, MUNCH, MUNCH.